The Hidden World of

Urban Farming

Operations with Decimals

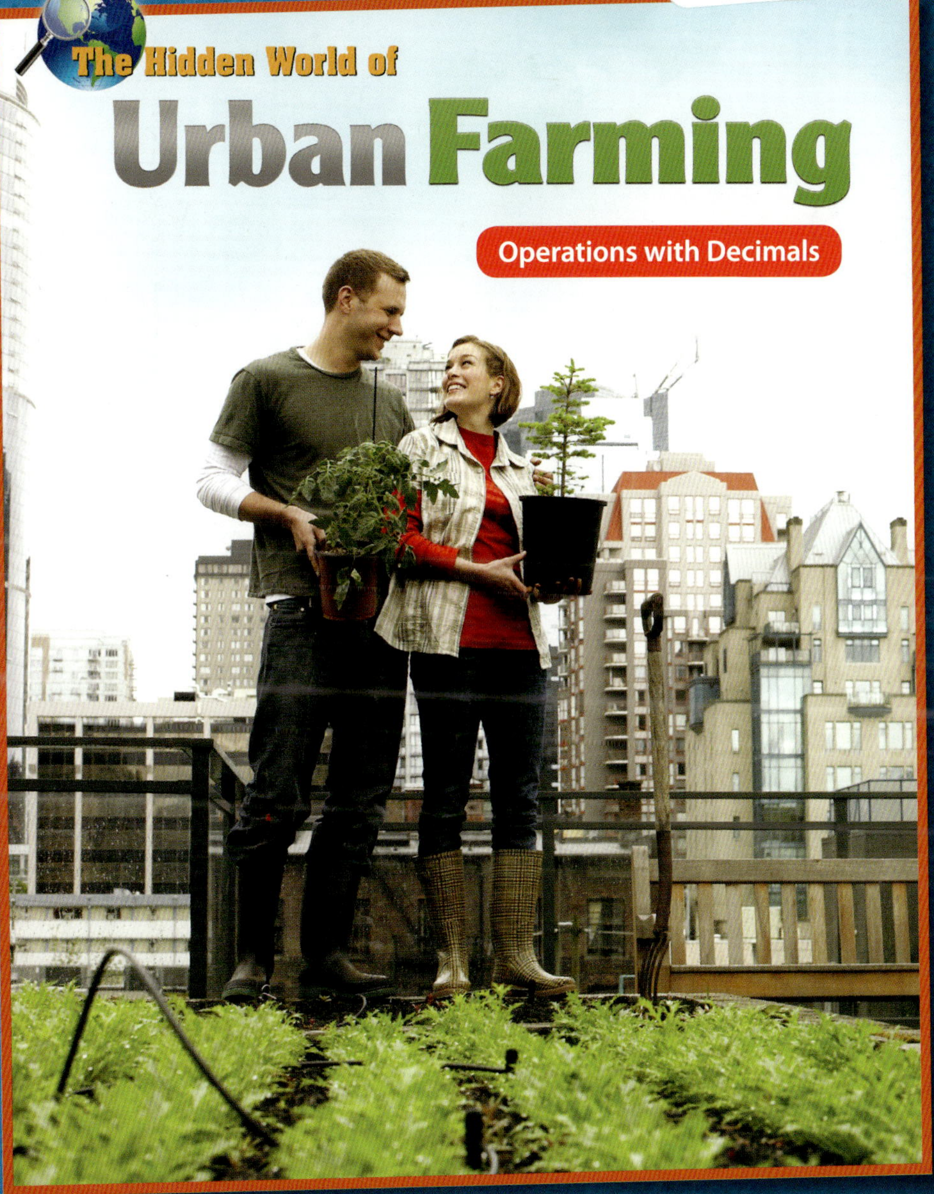

Roger Sipe

Contributing Author

Alison S. Marzocchi, Ph.D.

Consultant

Colleen Pollitt, M.A.Ed.
Math Support Teacher
Howard County Public Schools

Publishing Credits

Rachelle Cracchiolo, M.S.Ed., *Publisher*
Conni Medina, M.A.Ed., *Editor in Chief*
Dona Herweck Rice, *Series Developer*
Emily R. Smith, M.A.Ed., *Series Developer*
Diana Kenney, M.A.Ed., NBCT, *Content Director*
Stacy Monsman, M.A., *Editor*
Michelle Jovin, M.A., *Associate Editor*
Fabiola Sepulveda, *Graphic Designer*

Image Credits: p.12 MikeDotta / Shutterstock; p.22–23 Chicago Botanic Garden; p.24 Winslow Townson/Getty Images; p.25 (top right) Illustration by Fabiola Sepulveda; p.25 (top left) Holly Hildreth/Contributor/Getty Images; p.26 (bottom left) william87/ iStock; p.27 pio3 / Shutterstock; all other images from Shutterstock and/or iStock.

Library of Congress Cataloging-in-Publication Data

Names: Sipe, Roger, author. | Marzocchi, Alison (Alison S.), author.
Title: The hidden world of urban farming : operations with decimals / Roger Sipe ; contributing author: Alison S. Marzocchi, Ph.D.
Description: Huntington Beach, CA : Teacher Created Materials, [2019] | Includes bibliographical references and index. |
Identifiers: LCCN 2018051874 (print) | LCCN 2019005106 (ebook) | ISBN 9781425855222 (eBook) | ISBN 9781425858780 (pbk. : alk. paper)
Subjects: LCSH: Urban agriculture--Juvenile literature. | Mathematics--Study and teaching (Elementary)
Classification: LCC S494.5.U72 (ebook) | LCC S494.5.U72 S56 2019 (print) | DDC 635.9/77--dc23
LC record available at https://lccn.loc.gov/2018051874

Teacher Created Materials
5301 Oceanus Drive
Huntington Beach, CA 92649-1030
www.tcmpub.com

ISBN 978-1-4258-5878-0

Printed in Malaysia
Thumbprints.21254

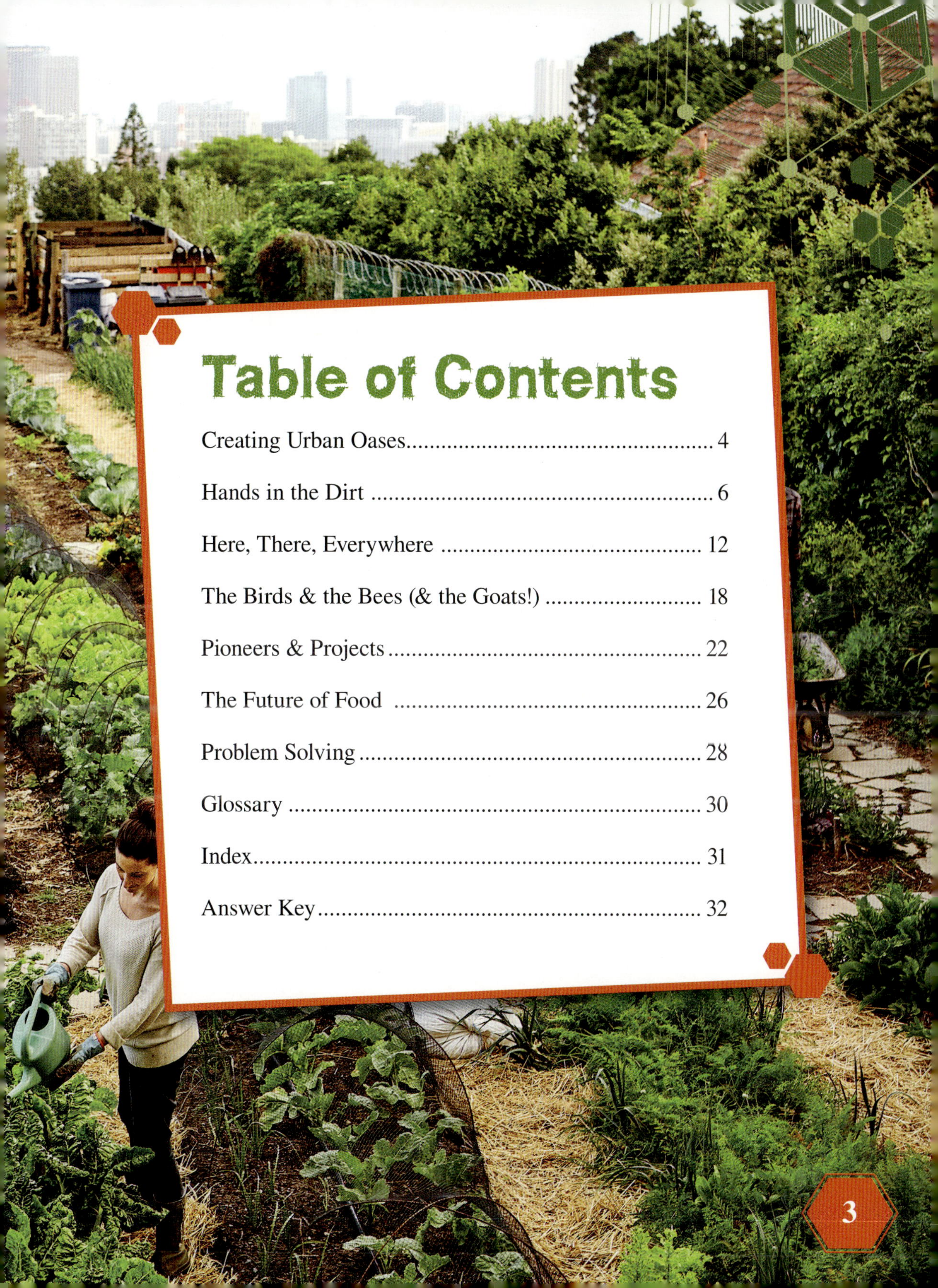

Table of Contents

Creating Urban Oases

Earth's population has doubled since 1970. Today, more than half the people in the world live in cities. That is a lot of mouths to feed in areas that do not have much space in which to grow food. Traditional farming methods can't continue to feed everyone. In fact, many people currently suffer from hunger. Plus, traditional farming methods are expensive. They use limited natural resources, such as oil, to move the harvest from the country to the cities. These are big problems. One solution might be urban farming.

Growing and harvesting food within city limits is the future of farming. It's already happening around the world. And urban farmers are producing *better* food. They are **composting** to make healthier soil and are using organic means to grow fruits and vegetables. These urban farmers are also planting on top of buildings instead of in fields. And they reuse and recycle materials to save money and resources.

Urban farming is more than just planting some seeds and reaping a harvest, though. It is a way of life. It helps urban dwellers be healthier and feel closer to nature while still being able to live and work in the city. While few people make a living as urban farmers, any **urbanite** can get involved. All they need are good soil, a few seeds, and a little bit of space.

A traditional farmer checks his crops.

Urban farmers check their crops.

Hands in the Dirt

Urban farming does not mean going to the local grocery and "harvesting" fruits and veggies by filling a shopping cart. People have to get their hands dirty and grow their food. Before they can plant any seeds though, they have to make sure the soil is healthy.

From the Ground Up

To begin a garden, the soil needs to be tested. Urban soil is not as healthy as the soil found in a country field. A vacant city lot that looks ideal for growing a garden might have previously had a home or building on top of it. That well-worked soil can contain high levels of lead and other **pollutants**.

A soil sample is taken and sent to a lab to see if it is safe to grow food. At the lab, scientists test the soil for its **acidity level**, the amount of **nutrients** it has, and any unsafe metals, such as lead. If the results are in the safe zone, the soil can be used to grow crops. The farmer will then prepare the garden by adding organic matter to the soil. If the results of the soil sample are not in the safe zone, the soil must be removed. This removal process can be costly, as the dirt has to be disposed of safely.

A person collects soil samples.

LET'S EXPLORE MATH

Scientists use the pH scale to measure acidity levels. If soil has a pH level above 6.5, any food grown in it absorbs very little lead. Imagine that you are a scientist testing pH levels of samples from different possible gardens. Which gardens would you recommend to planners and why?

Garden A: 6.55

Garden B: 6.15

Garden C: 6.49

Garden D: 6.62

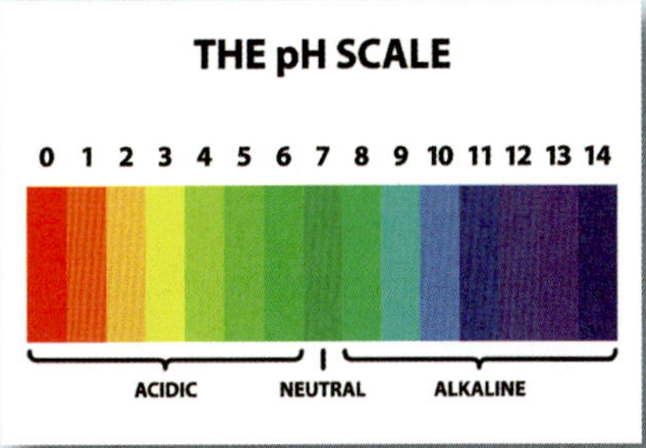

Raising Their Game

Many urban farmers choose not to use urban soil at all. Instead, they build their gardens in boxes placed on top of the vacant lots. These raised-bed gardens are rectangular and made of wood or other sturdy materials. A protective layer is put on the bottom of the box, and new, healthy dirt is dumped in. Urban farmers also use other types of containers to grow plants. Pots, crates, and other small containers are perfect for urban gardens because they are light, portable, flexible, and inexpensive.

Feeding the Soil

All soil used for farming must be healthy. Certain nutrients help produce healthy plants. Urban farmers can keep their soil healthy by feeding it with compost. This natural addition is made of organic matter, which has been labeled as either *browns* or *greens*. Browns provide carbon. They include dead leaves, branches, and twigs. Greens provide nitrogen. They include grass clippings, vegetable and fruit scraps, and coffee grounds. Urban farmers add browns and greens to piles in equal amounts. They also add water to provide moisture. With proper upkeep, the compost will break down into a rich, dark, dirt-like substance in a matter of months.

This cross-section of a compost bin shows browns and greens breaking down.

LET'S EXPLORE MATH

Urban farmers are happy to receive donated compost! Imagine that a landscaping company donates 12.2 kilograms of brown compost and a restaurant donates 17.66 kilograms of green compost to an urban garden.

1. How can you tell whether the total donation is greater or less than 30 kilograms?
2. What is the exact total weight of the donation?

Sowing Some Seeds

Once the soil is healthy and balanced, it is time to plant some seeds. While technically anything can be grown in an urban garden, some crops are better suited than others. Some crops, such as rice, require large amounts of water to grow. Rice is grown in extremely wet regions and is not ideal for urban farms. Grains, such as wheat, need a lot of room to spread out. They also require heavy machinery to be harvested. Grains are great for rural fields but not for urban rooftops.

Urban farmers have found the most success with crops that can be harvested several times a year, such as leafy greens and some herbs. Traditional vegetables, such as tomatoes, zucchini, and cucumbers, are also popular choices. They can be grown vertically to save space. Gardeners have even produced miniature varieties of certain melons, including watermelons, cantaloupes, and honeydews. Fruit that is grown on trees, such as apples, are a little more advanced as they take years to grow and produce fruit.

To keep pests away, urban farmers try to use organic substances and not human-made chemicals. These make the plants healthier. They also make the crops healthier.

Here, There, Everywhere

By using raised beds and containers, urban farmers have found new ways to grow crops. They are growing upward, outward, and every which way in between. Urban farmers can plant their crops just about anywhere.

They are working together in community gardens. They are planting crops that will grow up the sides of walls. They are even growing atop skyscrapers!

Neighborhood Goods

Apartment dwellers have to farm on a small scale. A lack of space limits them to having only a few plants on windowsills or balconies. To find more space, many people have started community gardens. At these shared open spaces, people are responsible for their own **plots**. They can grow whatever crops they desire, while some resources, such as water and compost, are shared.

These community gardens are often found in public areas, such as churches and schools. Some organizations or local governments also rent or lease their land to farmers. But to reserve a plot, an urban gardener has to contact the head of the garden well before springtime. Plots go fast!

People visit a community garden in a central square of Turin, Italy.

LET'S EXPLORE MATH

Imagine that a community garden is 422.64 square meters. Planners divide it into 12 same-sized plots for urban gardeners.

1. Planners estimate that each urban gardener will have a plot of about 42 square meters. Is this estimate greater or less than the actual size of each plot? Explain your reasoning.
2. How can you adjust the estimate to make it closer to the actual size of each plot?

People work in a community vegetable garden.

Time to Grow Up

Most urban farming takes place outside on level ground. Many creative urbanites, however, are finding that growing up is better. One form of vertical farming takes place indoors where crops are grown in stacks, one row on top of another. Instead of the sun, each level has special lighting systems called *grow lights* hanging above it. Instead of rain, the plants rely on watering techniques such as **hydroponics**.

You can't grow fields of grains vertically because they require a lot of space. **Root crops**, such as carrots, are also out because they grow under the soil, which tends to have high levels of lead. However, high-value and nutritious crops, such as tomatoes, lettuces, spinach, kale, and strawberries, are easy to grow vertically.

Outside walls can also be used to grow crops vertically. Urban farmers can place several small containers up the sides of the walls of their houses. The walls must receive some sunlight each day to make sure the plants get the nutrients they need.

This vertical strawberry farm is grown using hydroponics.

A farmer checks lettuce to see whether it is ready to harvest.

This lettuce grows in racks underneath grow lights.

The Sky's the Limit

Some cities have plenty of unused areas for gardens. However, in **densely** populated places, such as New York City, land is scarce. What is left is either too expensive for farmers to purchase or is shaded all day by tall buildings. This has some urban farmers reaching for the sky by planting their gardens on rooftops.

Rooftops are naturally flat spaces, high above the ground. This makes them perfect for capturing sunlight and rainwater. But before rooftop gardeners bring in containers and build raised beds, they must first call **structural engineers** or architects. They have to make sure the roofs are strong enough. All that dirt and equipment is heavy!

In addition to growing fruits and vegetables, these **green roofs** capture storm-water runoff and help keep buildings cooler. It's like the buildings are all wearing hats on hot days. Rooftop gardens also reduce noise and air pollution and provide homes for birds and other wildlife. Plus, they are way more attractive than dull gray roofs!

A gardener works on a roof garden in Hong Kong.

LET'S EXPLORE MATH

An apartment building's manager decides to create a rooftop garden and needs to tell the structural engineer the roof's exact area in square meters. He uses a diagram of the roof and calculates the area by multiplying. But he is not sure where the decimal point should appear in the solution. Use estimation to place a decimal point in the product. Explain your reasoning.

The Birds & the Bees (& the Goats!)

When most people picture farms, they probably think of animals. However, cows, horses, and pigs are much too big for rooftops and community spaces. Chickens, bees, and goats, however, are a different story. And many city folks proudly raise these animals!

Before deciding to raise any of these animals, urban farmers must check local zoning laws. Cities vary in what is allowed inside their limits.

Chicken Littles

A rooster's loud crow each morning would be a bad thing in the close **confines** of a city. In fact, that loud call is one reason why most cities do not allow them. The more **docile** and quiet hen, however, does not need a rooster, since she can lay an egg whether a rooster has **fertilized** it or not. If a rooster doesn't fertilize the egg, it will never form into a chick. But those eggs make a tasty breakfast for the city farmer. Depending on the breed, a hen can lay an egg about every 26 hours. For that reason, the chicken is the animal ***du jour*** of the urban-farming world.

These hens live in an urban area.

The Bee's Knees

Because they are tiny and easy to keep, bees fit perfectly into urban farms. Honeybees help gardens grow. They also provide a treat! Honeybees gather nectar from plants to make honey. In that process, they transfer pollen grains among flowers. This turns some flowers into fruits and vegetables. Bees then take that nectar back to their hives, where it is turned into honey. Bees make so much honey that humans can harvest some, and it doesn't harm the bees.

A beekeeper inspects bees and honeycombs.

LET'S EXPLORE MATH

Fernando helps beekeepers harvest honey from two hives at an urban farm. The first hive produces 1.361 kilograms of honey. The second hive produces 2.27 kilograms of honey.

1. Fernando calculates the total amount of honey. But his sum does not match his estimate, so he knows he made a mistake.
   - **a.** What do you think Fernando's estimate was? Why?
   - **b.** What is Fernando's error?
   - **c.** What is the correct total amount of honey?
2. How much more honey did the second hive produce than the first hive?

$$\begin{array}{r} 1.361 \\ +2.27 \\ \hline 15.88 \end{array}$$

Getting Your Goats

Some advanced urban farmers are raising dairy goats, especially miniature breeds, for milk. Besides drinking the milk, farmers use it to produce other dairy-based products, such as cheese and yogurt. Female goats, however, are not like hens, which don't need roosters to lay eggs. A female goat needs to be **bred** and have a baby each year to produce milk. Goats are also herd animals and prefer to be kept with at least one other goat.

Pioneers & Projects

Anyone can be an urban farmer. If you grow food within the city limits, you are one. Some urban farmers and their farms, though, are really breaking new ground.

Plant Power

In Illinois, the Chicago Botanic Garden's Windy City Harvest Youth Farm provides after-school and summer jobs with opportunities for growth! Every year, between 80 and 90 teens called "Youth Farmers" get a chance to work at three urban farms and one traditional farm. Planting, growing, tending, and harvesting their crops are big parts of what they do. So is having fun! They cook lunches for their fellow farmers using food they grow, go on field trips, and complete farm challenges. They also learn to work as a team and share the power of plants with others.

Youth Farmers in the program work on community service projects. For instance, they donate food they grow to food pantries. They sell their food in neighborhoods where it is hard to buy fresh produce. They also give cooking demonstrations and nutrition education classes. They help elderly people take care of their own gardens. Youth Farmers work together to do all this and more.

A Youth Farmer takes care of a planter in downtown Chicago.

Youth Farmers take a break from harvesting their crops at an urban farm.

Growing a Nation

Chicago has other farming success stories. It even has a garden at one of its airports that grows plants without soil! The plants' roots are misted with nutrition. This process is called **aeroponic** gardening.

Other cities are growing food too. People in Boston, Massachusetts, hit a home run with a farm on top of a baseball stadium. It provides fresh fruits and vegetables to the stadium restaurants. In Detroit, Michigan, people are turning unused land into acres of vegetables with more than a thousand urban farms. Oko Farms in New York City, New York, grows vegetables, fruit, and fish, which is called **aquaculture** farming. In Atlanta, Georgia, a mayor even created a special job called an urban agriculture director. The hope is to have more local food grown in the city.

Volunteers in Seattle, Washington, are creating an **edible forest**. Everything grown in the forest is free to pick and eat. The upper level of the forest includes fruit and nut trees. The lower level includes berry shrubs. They hope to help feed as many people in the city as possible.

A woman checks the vegetables growing at Fenway Park in Boston.

aeroponic gardening at Chicago O'Hare International Airport

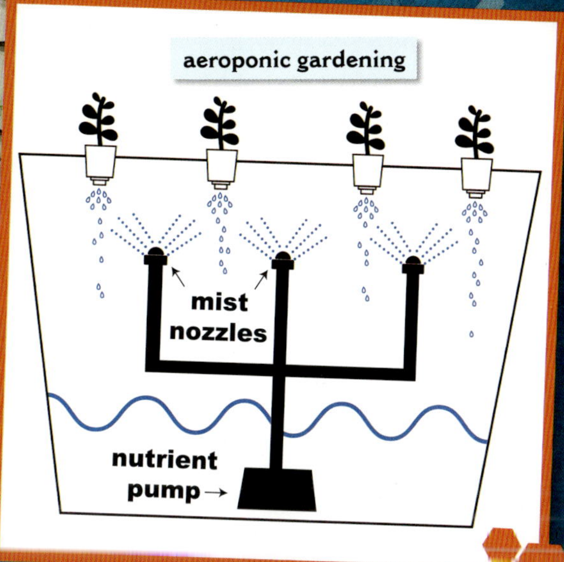

LET'S EXPLORE MATH

Some urban farmers donate their harvests to local food banks. Imagine that volunteers load 8 cargo vans with produce. Each van carries 453.59 kilograms.

1. Which operation would you use to calculate the total weight of the donated produce? Why?
2. Fifteen food banks equally share the total donation. About how many kilograms of produce can each food bank expect? Explain how you know the estimate is close to the exact amount.
   - **A.** 40 kg
   - **B.** 140 kg
   - **C.** 240 kg
   - **D.** 340 kg

The Future of Food

In time, urban farming will come out of its shadow. It has to. At present, more than 80 percent of the land that is suitable for raising crops is already in use. As rural farmland continues to disappear, the world's population continues to grow. By 2050, it is predicted that there will be more than nine billion people living on Earth. To feed everyone, cities will have to change. In the future, perhaps a raised-bed garden on a city lot will be as common as a red barn along a country road.

The potential of urban farming is limitless. Imagine a 30-story building built on a single city block, but instead of corporate offices, it has rows of harvestable crops. Artificial lights will act as mini-suns; advanced watering systems will act as rain. Architects are already dreaming up these futuristic plans.

Regardless of its scope and size, urban farming is here to stay. It is the future of food. You could say that it is a *growing* trend!

These walls at the 2015 Expo Milano were converted into vertical farms.

Future cities may look like this.

This vertical garden skyscraper is in Milan, Italy.

Problem Solving

Imagine that you are starting a new job as the urban agriculture director for a city. The owners of a vacant lot give you a diagram of their land and tell you they want to donate it. They think it would make a good urban farm, even though there is a square section of soil that needs to be replaced because it is too rocky. Use the diagram and the city's specifications to design an urban garden on the lot. Sketch your plan and write a summary for city council.

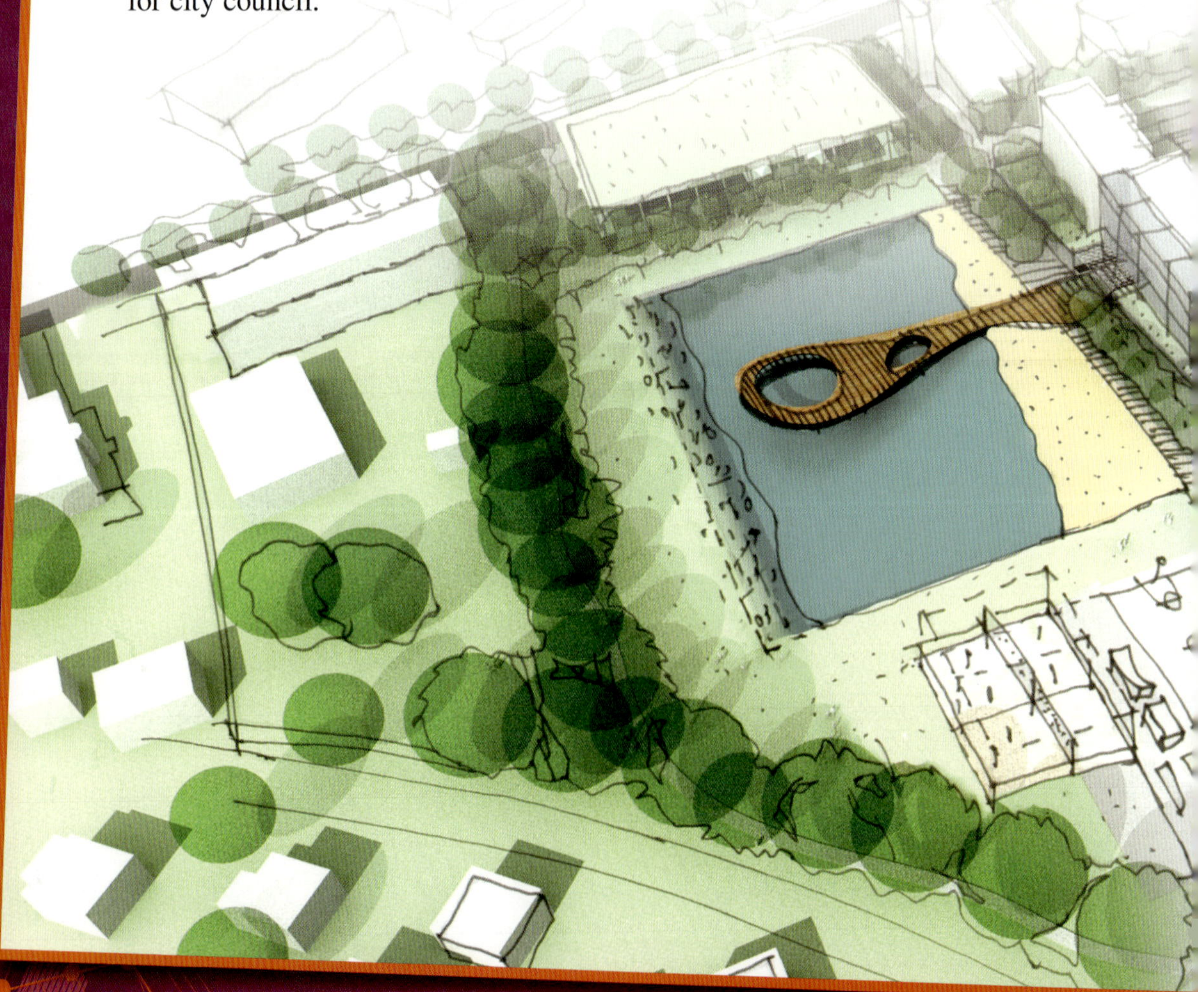

Vacant Lot (meters)

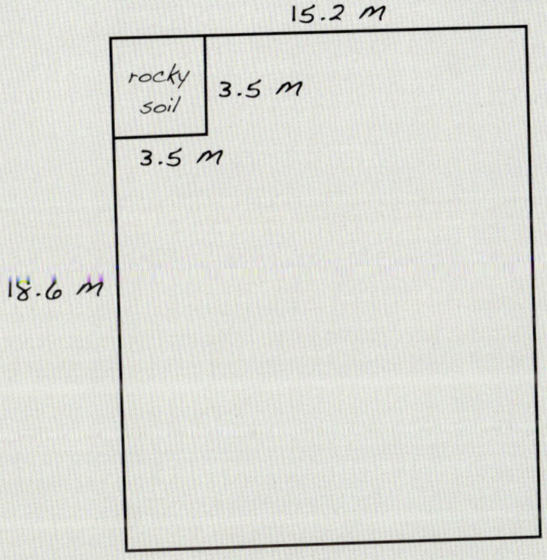

City Specifications

- ☐ Include at least 2 raised garden boxes. Each must be a rectangle or square. They may be different sizes.
- ☐ Include at least 4 equal-sized plots. These are plots that gardeners can sign up to use. Each plot must be a rectangle or square.
- ☐ Remaining area of the lot may be used as the agriculture director wishes.

Glossary

acidity level—the measure of acids in a soil on a scale of 1 to 14

aeroponic—a process involving growing plants in the air without using any soil

aquaculture—the raising of marine life, such as fish and sea plants, especially for food

bred—mated together to produce offspring

composting—mixing decayed matter of once-living things to be used for building healthy soil

confines—the edges or limits of things

densely—in a crowded manner

docile—easily controlled or led

du jour—French for "of the day"; meaning "popular"

edible forest—an area specifically planted with fruits, nuts, vegetables, herbs, mushrooms, and other plants for public use

fertilized—made an egg able to develop and grow

green roofs—roofs that are partially or completely covered with vegetation

hydroponics—the growing of plants in nutrient solutions

nutrients—substances that provide nutrition to help things grow or maintain health

plots—small areas of land

pollutants—things that make places or things dirty and potentially harmful

root crops—certain vegetables that grow underground, such as beets and carrots

structural engineers—people who work with the design and construction of structures, including buildings

urbanite—a person who lives in a city

Index

Answer Key

Let's Explore Math

page 7

gardens A and D because the pH levels are greater than 6.5, so the food will not absorb a lot of lead

page 9

1. less than 30 kg; 12 +17 = 29, and the remaining decimal parts of the numbers do not create 1 whole when added.
2. 29.86 kg

page 13

1. greater than actual size; If 422.64 is divided by 10, the area of each plot would be about 42 sq. m. Since there are 12 plots, the area of each plot must be less than 42 sq. m.
2. Estimates will vary. Example: *420 ÷ 12 = 35, so each plot is closer to 35 sq. m than 42 sq. m.*

page 17

910.48 sq. m; Explanations may include that 60 × 15 = 900, so 910.48 is the most reasonable answer.

page 21

1. **a.** Estimates will vary. Example: *3 kg because 1 + 2 = 3.*

   b. Fernando did not use place value to add the numbers.

   c. 3.631 kg
2. 0.909 kg

page 25

1. multiplication; Explanations may include that it is more efficient than addition because there are 8 equal groups.
2. C; Explanations may include that 240 × 15 = 3,600, which is close to the total weight of the donation (3,628.72 kg).

Problem Solving

Sketches should include at least 2 garden boxes and at least 4 equal-sized plots. Summaries should include areas of garden boxes and plots, area of remaining lot, and ideas for remaining area.